THIS BOOK BELONGS TO

_____

THANK YOU SO MUCH FOR YOUR PURCHASE, OUR VERY SMALL BUSINESS
APPRECIATES EVERY SINGLE CUSTOMER WE GET.

THIS BOOK IS FILLED WITH 100 PAGES FOR YOU TO DESIGN BEAUTIFUL
GARDENS.
 EACH PAGE HAS A BOX WITH GRID LINES FOR ACCURATE SKETCHING.
THERE IS ALSO SPACE FOR YOU TO WRITE IN YOUR IDEAS, NOTES AND
OTHER USEFUL INFORMATION.

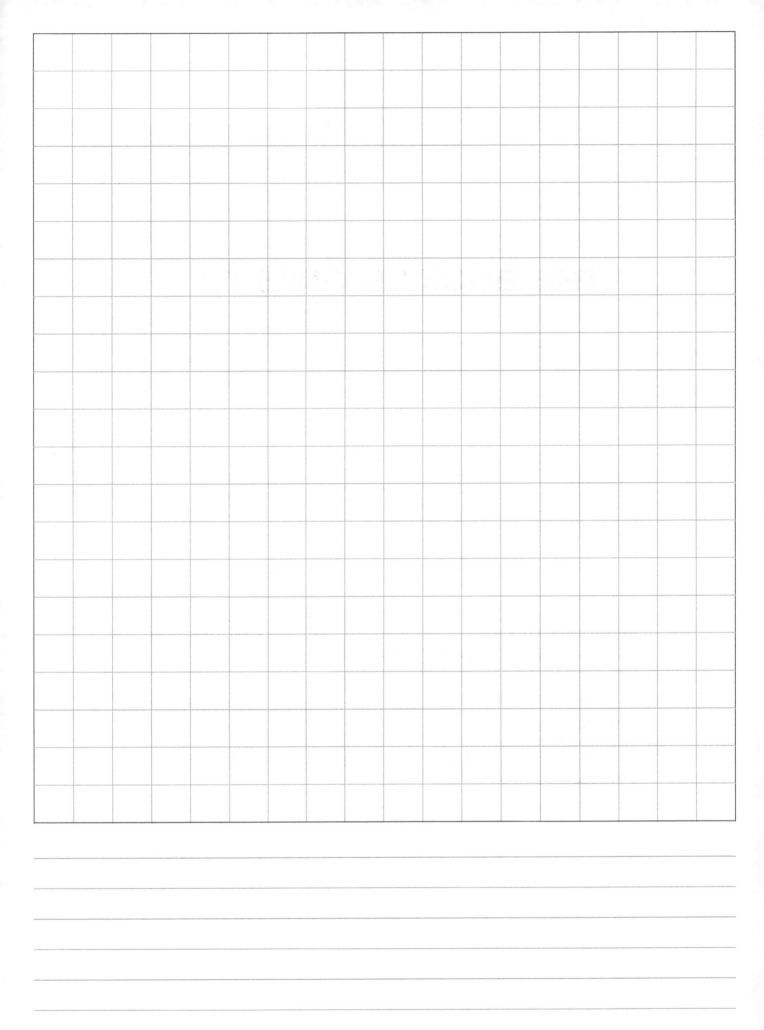

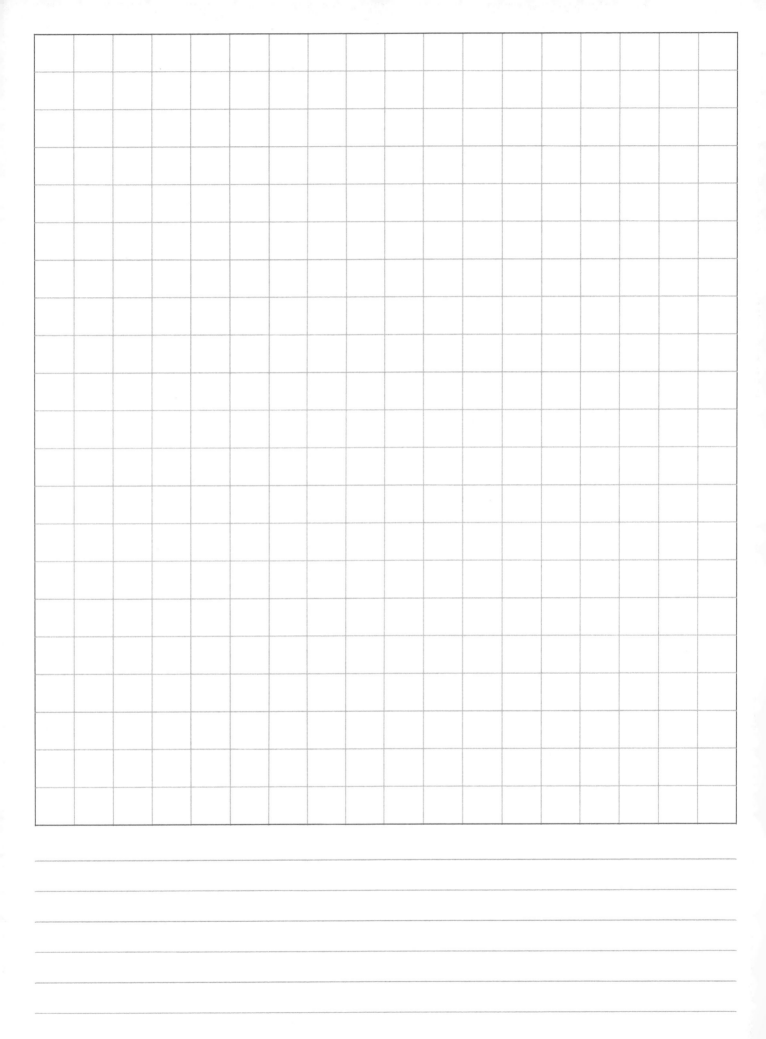

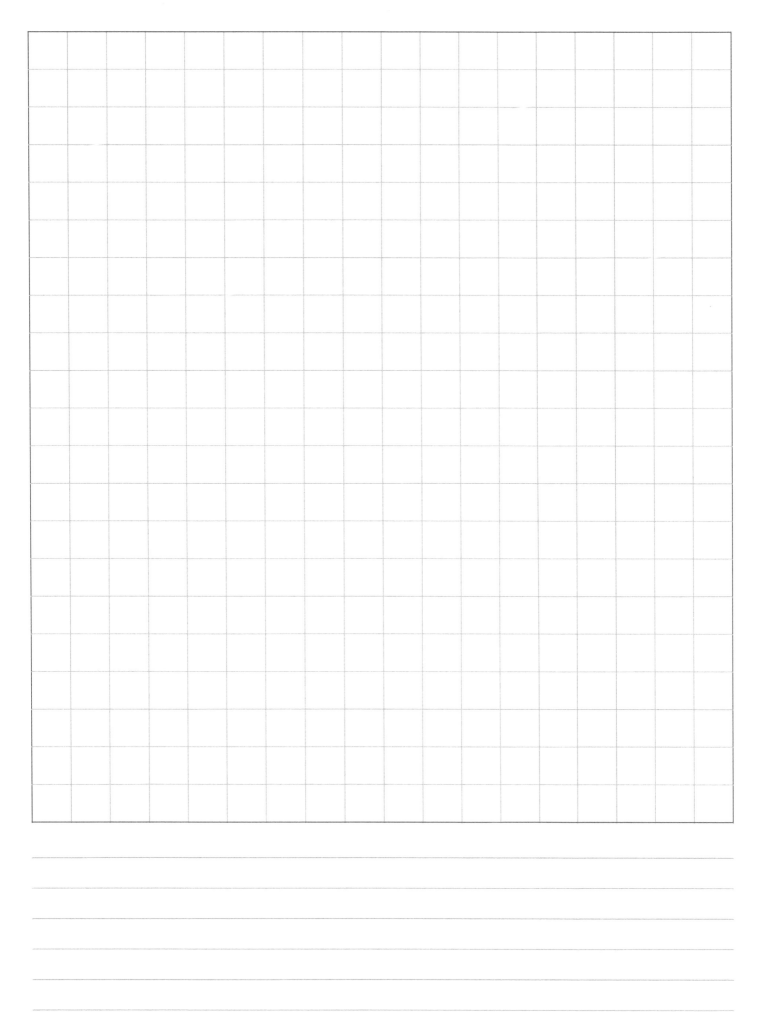

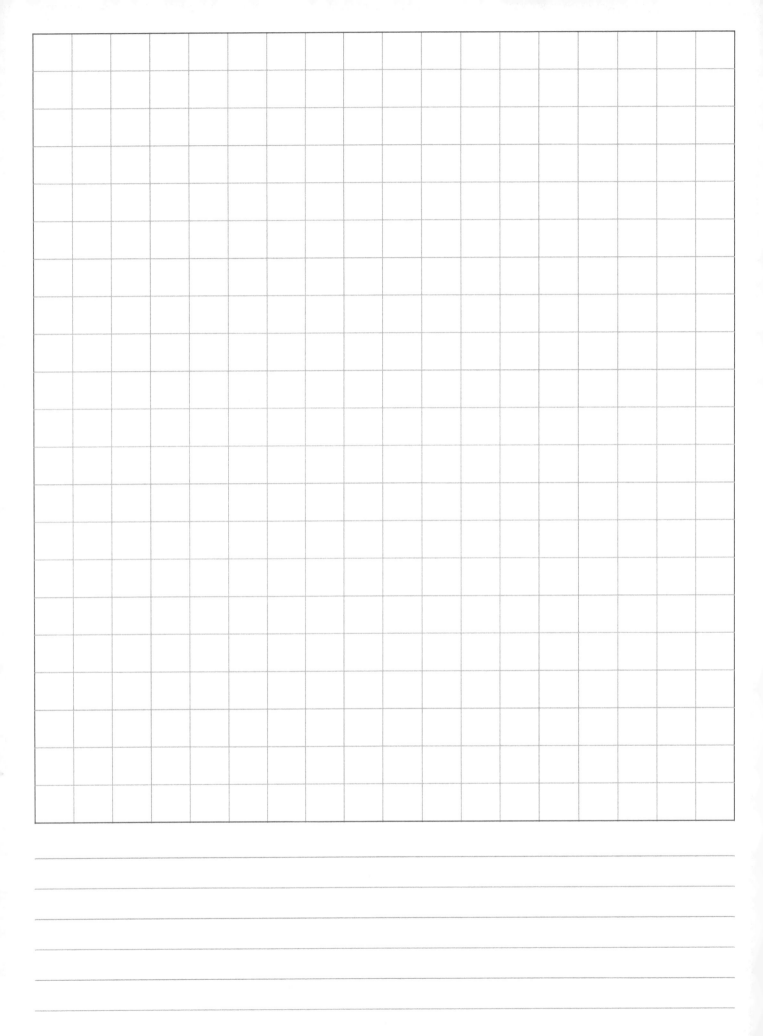

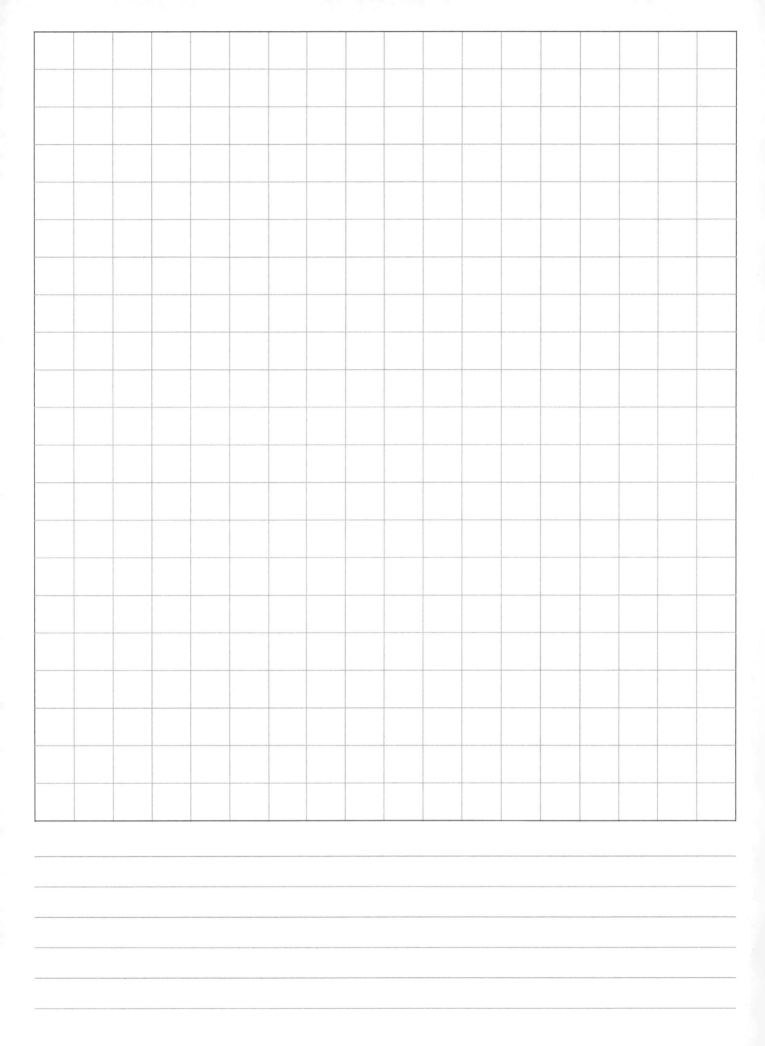

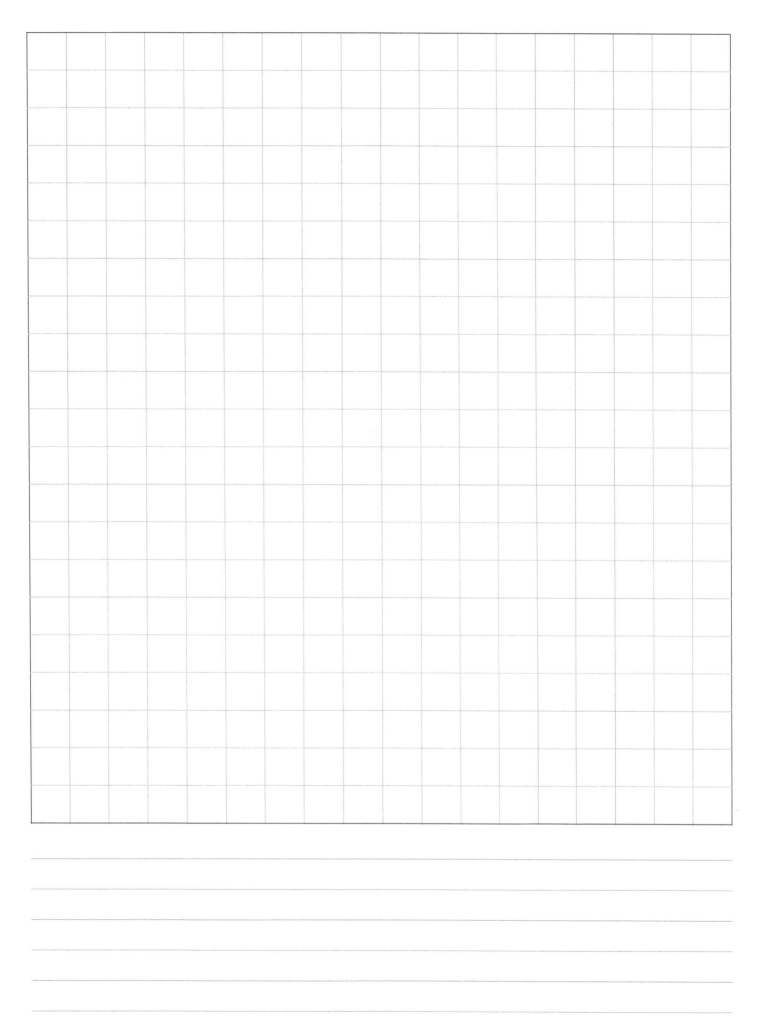

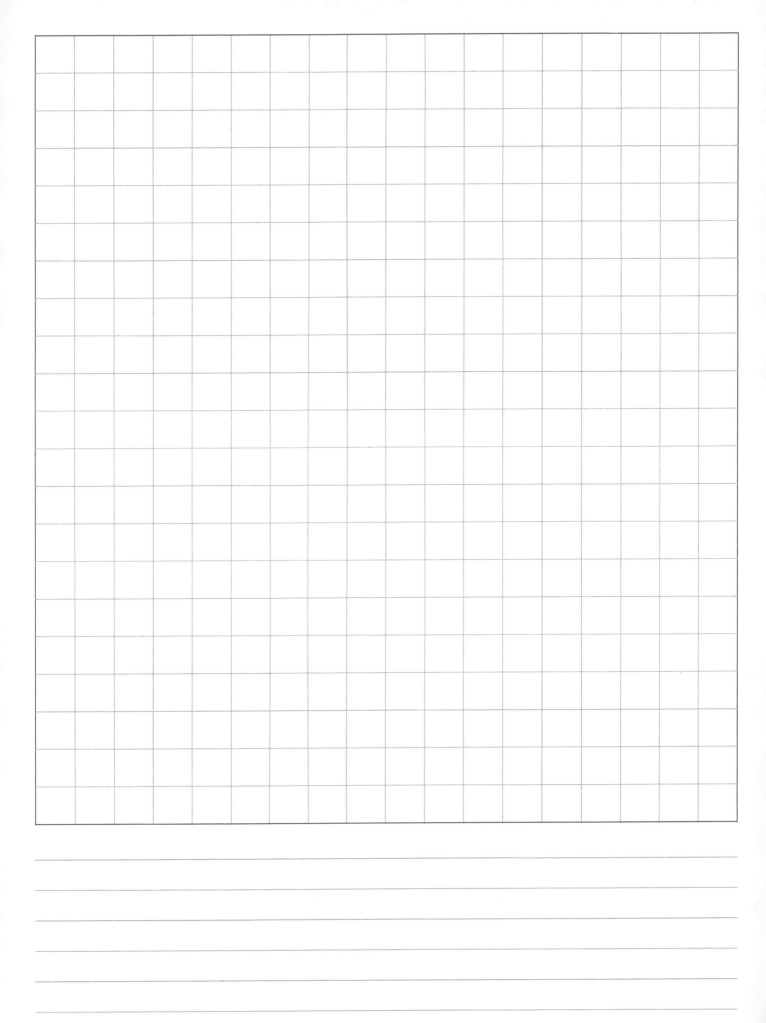

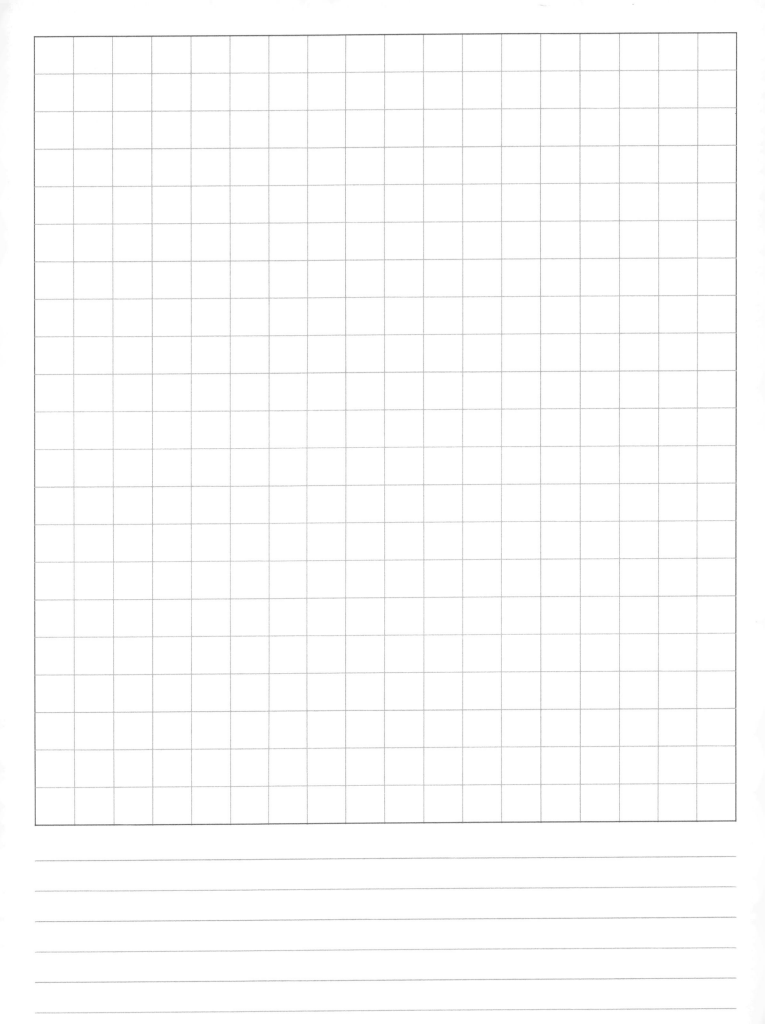

Made in United States
Troutdale, OR
04/28/2025

30951378R00058